Word

Of the Day

Love, Romance
& Inspiration
For Her

Tyrone

Rupert

Word of the Day
By Tyrone Rupert
Copyright: January, 2018

ISBN-13: 978-1983726316
ISBN-10: 1983726311

SOV Books
P.O. Box 2711
Downey, CA 90242
www.saintsofvalue.org

Printed in the United States of America

Introduction

Defining what love is. The journey for this condition is infinity. Beauty makes the heart weak. Money fulfills desires. Love grows within the spirit and starts with God. Truthfully, we Kings admire everything about the women of God. The Queens. For every second taken, close your eyes and imagine your special someone fulfilling your mental fantasy. Touching every gentle, polite and memorizing piece of your heart. Listen to the words. Press play and turn the pages. Glide through the paragraph and feel the phrases. Your time is simply amazing and I'm grateful to collaborate my pain, love and visions with you.

Love

Word of the day:

Love & Basketball

Scoring baskets is easy, but love points are difficult. I have to learn your offensive coordination. Can't reach, may cause a foul. Defense must be effective or substitution is mandatory. Took a charge with you falling on top of me. Game pauses. Technical. Mesmerizing position. One shot at me, second shot at you. No basket required. Soft wet lips, glacier clear eyes. The game is tied. Love controls are momentum. Let's score together. Overtime.

Word of the day:

Love

Love, outstandingly. Value everything. It's tough, but worth fighting for. Brings valued hearts together. Friends, family, strangers, significant other. Compromise everything. Love can hurt, become fatal, a triangle, or love at first sight.
Pick a direction and believe in your formation.

Word of the day:

'Fly'

Finally, Loving, You

Why do I need anything else when perfection rests under my nose? The joy of seeing you every morning is a dream to me. My partner, best friend till the end. Till death do us part, you'll always have my heart. A glow, I can't let go. Beautiful as a rose during photosynthesis. Chemistry so fateful, it never tangles. We work together on all angles. Pros and cons, you are my chest, I move your pond. Best decision giving to me. God blessed a gift I'll forever lift. Love you till I'm old and weak. My last breath, I'll sleep. Smile in my casket, heaven not tragic. You showed me the way to live for better days. I loved you, so I'm OK. Let us pray. Marriage is certain, just plan a day. I want you forever. I won't distance away.

Word of the day:

Rest

Watching you sleep is peaceful. There's no fighting, stressing, crying just joy for my soul. A warm feeling of happiness God's light shining on your spirit. Each breath travels smoothly as you smile. Dreaming of a wonderful place in your heart.

Rest you shall. Quiet is bliss.

Word of the day:

Connection

A connection takes two. Physical, mental, love, encouragement
You can be excited for the moment. But the connection can be
broken. False materials attached you. Judgement attacked you
Confused on what's reality, pleasure takes a burden. Pain runs
the dice. Is gambling worth the distractions? Stay connected.

Word of the day:

Passion

When a person is on your mind and makes you happy, that's an intriguing desire. To be with that someone always warm, gentle, respectful, intelligent. Finishes your completed sentences. verbally or mentally, satisfying my every breath. Fantasy and intimacy is imaginable but communication just as tangible. It strives for excellence, embraces self-awareness, role-model potential. You have that passion.

Word of the day:

Woman

Powerful, irresistible, phenomenal they are; the most precious part is seeing a beautiful smile, with a matching pair of eyes. Independence meets standards. Loving with intention to keep Some don't appreciate the value. They abuse, hurt, discredit, cheat. The one thing that made us, we hurt. Teachers, lawyers, Mothers; without your successful guidelines, we men are nothing! Thank you, sincerely.

Word of the day:

Miss

A memory is something spectacular. All events we encountered are phenomenal. As time goes by, the mind still wonders. Will I see you again? Sunset raises, the air is warm. I don't have you between my arms. Clock is ticking, heart is beeping. The wind is silent, my eyes are weeping. Up all night and don't know why, love of my life just passes me by. I see a shadow and no-one there. I miss you so much; just know I care.
Sleepless, singing, incomplete, missing....

Word of the day:

Feelings

Honestly, I just want to be happy. Living with a potential wife
and becoming a homeowner, husband, and be honored. Enjoy
life with my best friend. Create my own family and wake-up
with the two of you on my side. Very thankful. Travel the world
and capture each moment. Smiles, laughter, pleasure and the
unexpected. Marry the second most important woman in my
life. Blissful to have my mother and father watch this day.
Excited and pleased to change your last name. Live to watch our
children grow. Fight throughout the challenge with this
generation. We parents are the primary examples for their
future. Devoting all my energy for you and the children to never
face any sort of depression. As we age, trust and longevity
continues to function. I'll never stop loving you until I die.
Can you meet me there?

Word of the day:

'Lafs'

Love, At, First, Sight

Constantly on my mind. Sick, contagious, and memorizing.
You in my presence, exciting, resentful, angry and more. Our
attachment seems to never fragment. From simple walks to
lunch, you're an acquiring taste. Smile and tears, laughter and
fun with no fear. I wouldn't choose anyone else. Waiting
to hear your voice or a phrase, creates a smile with fulfillment
amazed. You're the one for me.

Word of the day:

Wife

She's everything. A friend, a co-worker, partner, and lover. Give all my strength to you. My back against yours. The opposite sex who loves her husband. Show you to the world and be proud of it. I'd kill myself for you. Not a moment to lose. Breathless without you. Your voice is my music. No app needed. Love turning you on. That smile, it's irresistible; the reason why I married you. Truest friend I know. No secrets, just honestly, love, and respect. I'll never leave you. Keep my ring on tight, but your love tighter. Goodnight and forever more.

Word of the day:

'Sum'

Smile, Under, Me

We work hard for time, warmth, and bounding. Yet it doesn't sum up. You provide equality at home, prepare meals, mobility and excitement. Amazingly lonely. Sliding across home base, you're tired of running. Someone cares for you. If the job's not fulfilled, you can smile under me. I'll hold you till time stops.

Listen and respect your mind, body, and soul.

Word of the day:

'Close'

Challenge, Love, Opposite,

Sex, Everyday

Magnets are hard to pull apart. Apply conflicting chemistry, they build a forcefield of distance. Grasping time is efficient. Help motivates energy balances while creating opportunities. Don't wait for suggestions. Challenge your mind and lead the way. Small gifts or arrangements have big effects. Take the wheel. Show how close you want to be. The appreciation will open avenues of joy. Communicate, listen, and respect. Keeps you one step ahead.

Word of the day:

'Toys'

Thinking, Of, You, Seriously

I try but can't stop. Every song, every moment makes me smile. I'm not alone at this. Your energy drives my day. No stress, no tension. You are my sun. Bright, funny, and blinded. Regardless of the pain, it's worth everything. The entire world needs your inspiration. We'll all be happy. I love toys.

Word of the day:

'AOL'

All, Over, Love

Love is so powerful. We have no control over the reactions we cause when activated. Under a spell, locked into faith, sometimes it's broken. Consequences are painful, even deadly. Can't turn back the hands of time. Either forgive or forget. Move forward and humble yourself. Never easy but manageable. Lead by example and respect all aspects. Be happy. Stay free.

Word of the day:

'Top'
Touch of Paradise

The island with clear blue water. Seafood and waves for
breakfast. Sounds nice. It's beautiful but your morning paradise
starts at home. Your kids, smiles, memoires, family. That's
everyday love, the development of life. Experiences that shadow
God's energy. Morning sun, first run. Night falls, so do we all.
Move in unity, smile in harmony. Not everyone has top
potential. But keep their faith high, praying in your mental.

Word of the day:

'Ring'

Resentful, Irresistible, Nicely, Glamorous

The details committed, acquiring ingenuous stone. Fatigue
days, sleepless nights. Beautiful colors, price unpaired.
Importance of choice, size, style, definition.
Secretly waiting for graduation. Time is perfection.
Perfect ring for the right woman.

Word of the day:

Falling

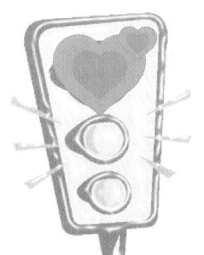

I can't hold you. Tired of fighting this emotion.
Even if the direction is incorrect, it's perfect.
The law of the land. Clueless, never. But I'm reminded
everywhere I look. Can't remove the intuition. Hurting and
excited for time. Unimaginable promises. Nothing fair. Free to
friendly fire but handcuffed on parole. Deep breaths are
challenging. Silent pain with nothing to gain. Realizing it's time;
discharge. Move forward and glance through the rearview. I can
barely see you. The light is still green.

Word of the day:

Happiness

Doesn't come from money or materials. That only gives you the moments. It starts within yourself. Waking up thankful and proud for another try. Fulfilling your destiny and knocking out your goals. Seeing your family and creating laughter. Occupying time correctly. Traveling the world and see its beauty. There's a piece of pie for everyone to try. Some sweet, some sour. Worth everything.

Word of the day:

'Hurt'

Hurting, Under, Rush, Time

Crisis events don't have understanding. Don't panic. Pray and give it to God. It's painful, frustrating and dreadful. Hold on and be strong. Your courage will better the outcome. Stand by him or her side. Stop asking why. Transfer your good spirit energy to the next. They're listening and being comforting by you. What goes down must rise above. Greatness is with you. Pray, breathe and continue supporting love. Believe.

Word of the day:

Joy

Jump, Over, Yesterday

Probably was just an awful day. Nothing going your way. Two steps forward, three steps back. Don't dwell, success happens each day. Push harder the next morning. A reboot is healthy. Never settle for a downfall. Progress starts with persistence. 40 days, 40 nights. A long road ahead but keep smiling. Focus with determination.

Word of the day:

'Held'

Holding, Emotions, Lonely, Dream.

Wishing I could hold you. The sun rises early morning.
Beautiful view to see your smile exposing your happiness.
As the day shifts, your shadows fade, while the moonlight trades
places. I only saw one image on the ground, realizing I was
alone. Listening to the waves while walking across the pier.
Silent while you're not near. All this empty space with no one to
share. Glancing at the moon, wishing you were there.

Word of the day:

'Gym'

Giving, You, Myself

I like the gym. Free your mind and pump iron. Each rep' brings a tremendous amount of pain and energy. Laying under 200-pound bench, I take a deep breath and push hard. The weights disappear and you become the equipment. Just when I begin to struggle, your inspiration pushes my sensation. Talking to me, smiling and coaching me through. Fatigue, sweat and tears.

I show no fear. All my ounces, miles earned.

You were there while I burned.

A beautiful, spiritual mirage.

Word of the day:

'Itch'

Incredible, Touch, Cherish, Harmony

When you're around me, I'm itching. No scratching involved. Just feelings. Wanting you in my everyday life. The time, laughter, precious moments together. An enjoyable relationship that's grateful forever. Fun fulfilling environment. Your presence starts and finishes my day. Impeccable smile, courageous attitude. Always excited throughout everything. You are the definition of love. The closer I get, the condition repeats itself. I might have an infection.

Word of the day:

'Mart'

Marriage, At, Right, Time

Don't get married because you're pregnant or your family says
so. Marriage starts with true love. Best friends fully devoted to
one another. Enjoy spending quality time, vacations, and family
extravaganzas. Trust is vital. A piece of paper doesn't change
the love you shared before. It's bridging the gap towards unity.
Equality justifies marriage success. Partnership is everything
if all strides point forward with nothing to look back at.
Understanding is visibly clear. Give it a chance, conversate.
When welcome, jump the broom. Love is a blessing.

Word of the day:

'Save'

Save, Anyone, Value, Everything

Watching a person go through depression is stressful, especially if they having suicidal energy. So much love given to keep them alive. A mother, father, teen-ager. It's a life. We must do our part and make certain death doesn't happen. Notice the signs. Check the environment. Watch the behavior. You are beautiful. We love you. You're not a failure. Life wasn't written to be easy. His life was given for you to live. Please trust and believe one last time. God is here with you. You're never alone.

Word of the day:

'Alt'

A, Love, Test

Just like a keyboard, love is buttons you press. The configuration is complicated. There's no instructions but right and wrong. The amount of work entitles happiness. Love yourself before you fall in love with your partner. Two loves can make it right. The vertebrae to your back. Support both aspects for an enchanting everlasting. The environment may judge, but that's the test. Still typing this love letter...

Word of the day:

'Spine'

Sensation, Passion, Intercourse, Naturally, Examined

Beauty shouldn't be this close. Married at sight, loving you so right. Smile for me tonight. I won't fight. My soul shall hold tight. Powers of God, I shall, I might love tonight. This hard fight in mind. I want to hold you till we wine. Red roses, skin soft, eyes frozen. Smiling sexy as we're posing. Locked lips, sweat drips. Rubbed hips, head dips. Time has frozen. Loud noises. Breathless. Second, charged and flexing. You're my gun, my only weapon. No second guessing. Loving me like the ocean sea.

I choose you, but you making love to me...

Sensation, Passion. Intercourse, Naturally, Examined.

Word of the day:

'Soy'

Start, Our, Year

I can't remove the pieces, but I want to join your puzzle. Mentally, I try to better myself for you, every day. From fitness to success. I want you to have me at my best. It's not a contest when love is the test. A quest to challenge, manage your universe. You can't see my vision but know it's clear. I have you in my ear. No fear, just want my dear. From calls to texts. A visual smile is next. A dream so far-fetched, I'll stretch my neck. Potential, not so simple. Amazing, starring at your dimples. I keep you in my mental. You're so gentle. Sweet with all desires, you are the flame to my fire. Earth and wind. For you, I'm all in.

Word of the day, Jot

'Just, One, Time'

Alone with you, finally. Thinking how nice this opportunity can be. Not rushing to any point but just staring at memorizing beauty. Room for love, passion which starts with fashion. Removing your clothes with my eyes. Very wise and anxious for a surprise. Ignition started and the tank is full. The drawback of fatigue puts you to rest. My heart just dropped out my chest. Can't fight a silent stress. Your company is my 'blessed.' One day, I'll have you as mine. For now, I'll inhale these herbs and drink on this expensive wine, waiting for time. Just a crime because you're so fine. Dose off till I'm sleep, I'm already blind. Wake up to the morning shine. I'll be fine.

Word of the day:

Why

Wanna, Hold, You

Willing to make you feel like a woman should. Love you
unconditionally. What's so wrong about that? Why push a good
man away? Holding that emotion which broke your heart in the
past. We're not the same. Even though you don't respond with
action, there's movement in your eyes. Amazingly bright with a
smile so white. You never want me to leave, yet feeling alone
with you next to me. I provide, strive and make time. Stop on a
dime to see your smile every time. Options start becoming
obstacles. Our mission impossible. Help me understand.
I can't walk away empty when you block the door. I wanna'
explore your world. I'm a tourist. I know this location but not all
avenues. Shows me the hotspots. Where's the best view?
Hopefully it's just you. Draw a map. Lay down your foundation.
Pin point your angles. Include me in your radius. I'll move 90%
and wait for your 10's. Ten minutes, hours, days, weeks, years.
Whatever it takes to have your heart and tears.
I'm always here, my dear.

Word of the day:

'Jam'

Jump, After, Me

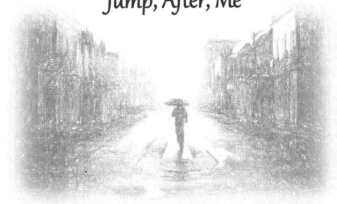

A man with an exciting heart loves you deeply, but is blinded by trust. A new picture with astonishing solutions creates smiles daily, even with the pain written on the wall. Never lets you fall. Visual dream turned reality. Two-sided technicality. Bumps in the road cause the vision to explode. Waiting on reactions and satisfaction. Trapped in a hole, we try to reach the same goal. Planting your legs on my shoulders, lifting yourself to freedom. I'm left behind and alone. You are my home. Dark, cold with no tools. I'll find a way to grab your heart before I lose. If I die here, I lie here. If I escaped, I'll never be late. Believe the fate. I'm in too deep in love, you see. Under these conditions ...
Will you Jump after me?

Word of the day:

Candle

Aroma just as pleasant as it is attractive. Placing you in different environments, constructing a balanced mood. Your timing is perpetual. Anxious, emotional and ready to strike you out. Flame starts at the top. As the conversation burns, the slower we breathe. Having you beneath me is a journey beyond dreams. Soft hair, warm bodies, eyes of heaven, fantastic anatomy. Body language is a silent cry. Tipped you over, darkness arrives. Wax is melting away. Painful drops, screaming tongue. No more time for you, depleted one. Gone and never forgotten. Your attention has me plotting. Beautiful, hot and a handful, my lady. Her name's Candle.

Word of the day:

'Yet'

You're, Everything, Tonight

Wish you were with me. Knowing you think about me, our circumstances have compromises but I'll risk everything. Your breath is my oxygen. The smile creates my 'humble.' Holding you is just right. Small appetizer with various choices. Laughter, kisses and endless wishes. A starry night I can't finish. For you I replenish. Your small hand holds a grown man. A pair of feet through the sand with my number one fan. We never make plans. Always happy where we stand. Vibrations from your heart beat, love so high we can't sleep. Emotions to deep, you smell pleasantly sweet, an amazing treat. Crying because you're so beautiful. Hurts to watch you leave. Knowing I don't have you doesn't mean one day I can't achieve.

Just watch and see. Pray and believe. Your heart is everything I need. Just one bended knee and a father's blessing. Added an island, dresses. Long speech confessions. Death do us part. 'Friends' is where we start. One plus two equals three. Accept my name and begin our new family. Trust is key. No obligations and conspiracies. Just you and me. Plant the seed and the reactions shall feed. Lovely indeed. Musical symphony.

Word of the day:

'Slow'

Sweet, Love, Overly, Wonderful

No rush for something sensational, smooth and grateful. Overdose with your love even though it's killing me. Trading smiles and conversations, you're always on time. Forever in my mind. Feel so fictional because you're so perfect. Every day I receive a new gift. You bring a different presentation without a buffer. Loving your steam. High clarity definition. We have pictures. Yet the moments are spectator. Remarkable bond like grandparents. Listening to your voice, very soft and influencing. Skipping breakfast to receive a lesson. Love at first sight. Beautiful and bright like the sky. Jaw dropping when I see you cry because I'm not standing by. Love's a terrific ride. Start slow, hold tight, then glide. You'll be surprised.

Word of the day:

'Kiss'

Kissing, Is, Something, Special.

A pause panics the heart. Is everything right? How's my breath? Does she want to? Does she like me? Millions of options racing through my mind. Nothing to rush. She's so beautiful. Knowing you for years and realizing this expression doesn't happen on its own. The closer you become, the intensity is powerful. Touching your face slightly, as I lean in. Darkness is slight, blinded with closed vision. Waiting patiently for your softness. Breathless connection. Warm, tasteful and at ease. As our eyes begin to open, behind forms a smile. Cheese. Very pleased to have you next to me. This moment will forever be grateful to see. Having your heart against me kissing the memorizing infinity. Times of our century. Thinking was it meant to be.
The moment of clarity.

Word of the day:

Baseball

Been striking out for years. Trying to find a way to understand your pitch. Taking steps to this base. Preparing for a change-up. As you release the throw, my aggression wants a home run. But with a bunt, I know you can tag me out. Striking the ball into fair play, I finally passed first base. A different position of involvement with you. Interaction very fulfilling. Seeing we are rivals, more or less, it's survival. Even though I lost the season, playoffs game, my heart has won your finals.

Champions celebrate together.

Word of the day:

Wind

The breeze that keeps me close to you. Silent whispers talking in my ear. Sometimes it gets cold. But I know you're all around me sending me signs to follow. Knocking the pen off the table towards a pad, I jot down my thoughts of you. Ink fading out, racing to purchase another. Driving comfortable with my eyes lowering, a force of energy lifts me awake. Thankful for your sake. Finalizing this letter, realizing I have no address destination. A detour down to the peer. Consuming the remains of the red wine, seducing this love note into the glass. Looking back at the past. Attached the top, tossed to the future. Whoever you are out there, let the wind guide this love toward to your heart. If you hear the message, it's not silent. Follow the pattern. We both can see the moon. The glass may show up one beautiful, cold afternoon. If there's nothing to read, at least the wind guided you to me. Invisible love, indeed.

Word of the day:

Gone

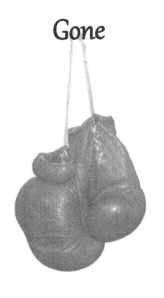

Why do I have to lose you? I put so much energy into inspiring you to be great, my buddy. Staring into this grave, lifting this shovel and dirt. Pouring the tears and dirt on top of you. It's only been a couple of years that we had. My soul is terribly sad. I remember the first encounter. Watching the struggle and fights but you never quit. Learn to build strength and strive to your excellence. Time is so short on this Earth. I shall celebrate everything that reminds me of you. The sun for smiles, rain for drops of compassion and sounds for laughter. I know you're not dead but in a distance space. Your memory will never be erased or misplaced. My heart will continue to race for us. Believe and trust. You're everything under the sun. A plus.

Word of the day:

'Fog'

Forgiving, Often, Grateful

Some actions lead to pain. Misguided aggression that violates your emotions. Hard to see through the cloud. Before you strike at the situation, find an enhanced view. Ponder responsibly. Relive yourself, then welcome the solution with your independence. As the vision begins to clear, anxiety shifts down a gear. Balance is gained with cheer. Thankful to forgiveness, grateful to show the given. We are only human. We are the living. To love each all, even when we fall. Keep loving through the fog. I'm here to help you, even while you crawl.

Word of the day:

Path

The remaining memories of us. Looking in the mirror, smiling. Seeing the images projecting from my vision into this wall. Viewing harmony at its finest. Great people work together. We once said, "We'll be forever till the bucket falls." Painting around the hurt, brushing off the mistakes. Dipping into the white paint, symbolizes a pure heart. Splashing all over you, glowing and happy. Red is the background. Worst when it enters your eyes. My heart is falling off the planet. Just breathe. Poured an entire bucket of yellow. I need heaven right now. I know she loves me. Please don't leave me. Rushing for paint and all I have is empty buckets. Final color is black. Eyes opened to darkness. This portrait was materialized through the exterior. Art's beauty.

Word of the day:

Smoking

When I first saw you, I didn't know what to think. I placed you on my lips, sparked a flame and inhaled deeply. Muscles relaxing, clouds exhausting. In disbelief, you treat me unbelievably. Knowing the consequences, I can't always have your time. I think of you countlessly. You make life flawless for the moment. Too bad you always fade away.

Word of the day:

'Polls'

Presents, Of, Love, Loyalty, Special

Love is an exquisitely packaged gift. The outside is a force of
urgency. Ready to unwrap, to discover the glowing benefits.
Analyzing a disfigured structure, I must understand your
beginning. Judgmental is not fundamental. Holding onto you
since you entered my life. Removing layers of elegance after time
moves forward. A connection so powerful my heart skips a
pulse. Channeling through the surroundings of replicas.
My soul only inhales your presence. Visions may one day be
available to me. A delivery involving letters of three.

S,H,E.

Love between you and me.

Inspiration

Word of the day:

Bridges

Some people like bridges. They/re big, wide, long, narrow. The view is phenomenal. Exercising on them is tough. Very steep, bumps on the road, with no time limits. Fatigue is intimate. Self- control takes training. Can't rush the performance. They can't speak but it hurts you physically. If walls could talk.

Word of the day:

Drivers' Ed

Some don't appreciate the value of a car. Beautifully crafted
with a design language only architecturals comprehend.
Initially, the test run "favorite." Wind blowing in your hair,
music up, feeling fresh. Next payment and relationship builds.
Daily or monthly maintenance, expenses, travel, emotions
change. Time progresses, new engine on market. Vehicle
controls your break communication. It talks to the driver,
5-star education, exceeds all expectations. Jumping into the
future carrying hurdles of advancement or maintaining a lease.
A valid tender.

Word of the day:

Beauty

Beauty is not something you purchase. Yet those who do become ugly. Self-love is no longer passionate. Wigs, makeup, surgery overtake the mind. The object you're becoming is now for affection, attention, desires, temptation. Higher standards are beautiful. Completing your education, accomplishing your goals, dreams, and believing who you are from within. Watching the sun rise while smiling in this life, is simply beautiful. False images, impersonators, materials, money can't fix the 'self.' Hard work, guidance, perseverance and faith will outshine all obstacles ahead.

Word of the day:

Face

Your face rejoices my inner being. Eyes vivid as the sun.
Glancing your direction opens a path for success. Natural skin
resembles a taste of pure diamonds. Contagious style, elegance.
Face, Admiration, Concur, Everything.

Word of the day

Help

Help is not just an action. Help doesn't have a price. It's not a
donation. Help comes from the heart. We help those in need.
From a bad day to an addiction. A hand can save anyone.
Jumping to grab a child from the street, risking your own life.
All we see is that amazing smile on his/her face. There's no fear.
Help is love.

Word of the day:

Soo

Seeing other options is a factor. It can lead to a significant light at the end of a tunnel. Open up opportunities. Or be a healthier gateway to a new establishment. Applications can be applied anywhere in your life. An occupation, relationship, family, study, or self-discipline. We choose the path in which we follow.

Word of the day:

Mirror

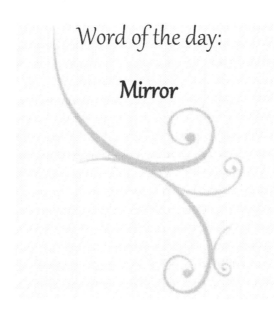

The mirror is perfection. Has its advantages for sight, distance and reflection. Character changes when being evaluated. Fixing imperfections, attire or imagination. Outside the mirror, your view is open, not trapped in that window. Everything evolves around you. Walking or driving, business, or arriving. Life doesn't stop. The next encounter with reflection, get confused with misdirection. Your image is outside the window.

Keep moving. See your faith.

Word of the day

Pencil

Water, life and sun started it all. Just like wood, we bound, we're strong, and brake. The smallest expression provided the most effort. Freedom to write, protest, draw and vote. Our voices express the same element. Pain, aggression, attention, rights. The pencil brought people together, manifested through education. Author, architects, artist, poet, director. Small tools used to advance the future.

Word of the day:

Peace

We will never have peace. It starts within our souls.
Understanding we are one. No color, no race, no flag. Just
humanity. Filter the noise of destruction, violence, war and
welcome love. Love is peace. One voice, one hand ...
has changed our lives eternally.

Word of the day:

Self

My life is uncompleted. Very talented with the hands God provided me. Trusting the window of faith to push blessing our way. Within the soul, it quits forcing itself across my mind, turning me left. Negative energy among family and friends pushes it further. Positive energy provided by a ring of intelligent individuals strives my heart. My clock's not done but self-improvement is always welcome. If I'm quiet, just know I'm focused on success not distance. Time to fade away. Hit nothing but bottom and bounce to the top.

Word of the day:

'Fear'

Fight, Establish, Awareness, Reason

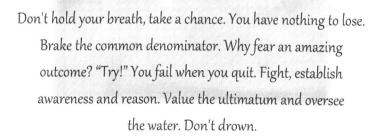

Don't hold your breath, take a chance. You have nothing to lose.
Brake the common denominator. Why fear an amazing
outcome? "Try!" You fail when you quit. Fight, establish
awareness and reason. Value the ultimatum and oversee
the water. Don't drown.

Word of the day:

Date

Orientation with superior first impression. Hair, cologne, hygiene, apparel. Communication and location. Time and labor adjusted for this exciting moment. Build emotion as you drive. Weeks of network messaging. Thoughts cycling anxiously. Finally, close the door, walk up, take a seat. No date. Only person you need to impress is yourself. Self-gratitude and success bring aspirational individuals. Love to last a lifetime.

Dream, Admire, Time, Everlasting.

Word of the day:

Smile

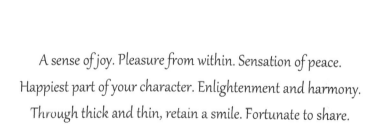

A sense of joy. Pleasure from within. Sensation of peace.

Happiest part of your character. Enlightenment and harmony.

Through thick and thin, retain a smile. Fortunate to share.

Elevate your surroundings.

Sweet, Memory, Incredibly, Lush, Ending.

Word of the day:

Drive

Goals and determination create a unique drive. Logical verbal conveyance, futurist visions and independence. Create a healthy core. Steps of progress. Slow or fast paced, effort is equality. Patience is key. Your heart establishes the drive.

Dream, Recognize, Impulsive, Value, Energy.

Word of the day:

Sniper

At war times, you are the MVP. Your sight down my scope has me breathless. So, focus with precision. You are my target. From 100 yards to a meter. I can't pull the trigger. Trained to kill, I cannot destroy beauty. My heart pumping, focus is blurry. I smile while my reflection shows a red-dot on my skull. I take one last breath and whisper, "I Love You." Shot down to save you, hoping one day, one mission, you save and love me.

Word of the day:

Fumble

You are the quarterback, running-back, wide receiver. Everyone
wants to hit you. From temptation to resentment. Hold on tight.
Grasp firmly. Continue to showcase affluence. Leadership
hurdles over deficiency. Pressure is active daily.
Success is immortal.

Word of the day:

Exit

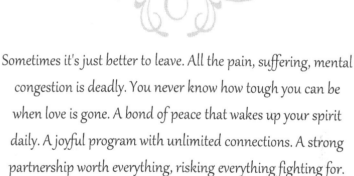

Sometimes it's just better to leave. All the pain, suffering, mental congestion is deadly. You never know how tough you can be when love is gone. A bond of peace that wakes up your spirit daily. A joyful program with unlimited connections. A strong partnership worth everything, risking everything fighting for. A light, I would go blind for. A feeling never expected to repeat itself. The chapter I cannot close.

Emotional, Xcape, Irritating, Truth.

Word of the day:

Gift

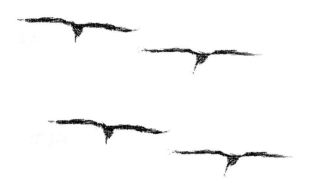

Money nor presents represent the message. Thought process and time is honorable. Running a marathon, donating blood, fighting cancer. It all fits the same cause. A gift of life shares with the forbidden. A generation of homo sapiens with defects granted, hearts are strong, faith is God. Giving, individuals, faith and trust keeps our world alive. There's no future if we quit the HELP. Represent your gifts.

Word of the day:

Sup

Every equivalent step ahead has its benefits. Financial compensation welcomes upper-class responsibility. New task, more demands, enhanced pressure. Fighting the success makes you appreciate the outcome after the pressure given creates a responsible, knowledgeable, and honest person. Maintain self-discipline, proficiency, acknowledging all doors are open. **Success, Under, Pressure** is up to self. Inhale or fade away.

Word of the day:

Lost

Really don't know anymore. Lifeless without love. I see you, I'm happy, then we part ways. We have situations, but the heart knows everything. Around you, everything gets pixelated and I just have you. A smile, a vision and peace. The dream is not the same. Deja vu is on repeat. **Love, Opposite, Sex, Tremendously.** It's not luck. It's destiny ... till tomorrow.

Word of the day:

Loyal

Submitting only to you. Your go-to, your best friend, your partner in crime. Nothing else is equivalent. Creates a mature relationship. When you fall, he/she picks you up, removes the tension off your shoulders. Evaluate time for you. Dating, vacations, events forever enhancing. Never looking for trouble. The perfect balance of true harmony. Can't live without you ... my internal lifeline.

Word of the day:

'One'

One, Night, Event

Some nights we can't reflect memory. Lights, drinks, flairs, smiles, just an amazing time. Energy is flowing, music is live, bodies are wildin'. But responsibilities are turned down. A side of you wants to orchestrate activities of such. Comprehension is staggering. You mind is turned off. All it takes is one dive. Swim toward life's ocean. We only get one chance. Positive outcomes overcome the negative. Keep the life jacket on and share your donut for the next drowning soul.

Word of the day:

Vocabulary

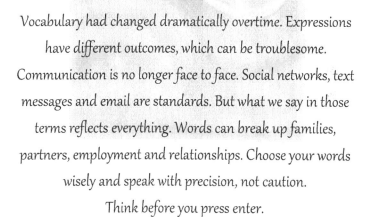

Vocabulary had changed dramatically overtime. Expressions have different outcomes, which can be troublesome. Communication is no longer face to face. Social networks, text messages and email are standards. But what we say in those terms reflects everything. Words can break up families, partners, employment and relationships. Choose your words wisely and speak with precision, not caution.

Think before you press enter.

Word of the day:

'Rain'

Romantic, Attention, Incredibly, New

Rain doesn't come from mother nature, it's within you. That fresh start of intimacy. Physical aspect, appearance, agenda and direction. Vibes that channel your challenges for communication. Building a short-term relationship for a life's journey. A job which requires no money. Priceless time and beautiful opportunities. Appreciate every drop given and you shall receive it in return. Rain is pure. Taste it.

Word of the day:

'Font'

Fussing, Over, Nonsense, Tension

Don't collaborate in the same room. Ready to quit. Sleepless nights, headaches, not eating, lack of memory. With no direction of fixing the problem, tension remains a factor. It's in the air. The easiest part is to not focus. Not being responsible. Outcome will never level. Pull yourself apart and fix one another. Figure out the difference and see if it's worth remaining together. Balance the good with the bad. See what chart is more effective. Check the command grounds. If it's not worth it, respect your departure and let go. But if you're willing to go twelve rounds, stay in the ring. Might not be able to see clearly, may be hurt, but it's worth your life's perspective to have love.

Word of the day:

Intuition

That feeling of happiness, confined deeply inside. The urge to remove yourself and zone out. Wrapping your hands around the body, staring into your hazel eyes. Grasping through your hair, inhaling the amazing perfume. So many directions to choose, each path is positive. Confused, lost but fierce in finding love. Never want to lose your sight. No one else matters. What do you want? Where do we go? Our left shows a boat, our right displays a plane. Materials don't matter as long as I have your lane. Your hands meet mine. My faith with you is at all time.

Word of the day:

'Run'

Running, Under, Neighbor

Relationships have history. Amazing times, beautiful stories, anger, lessons and more. We change like the weather. Rainy days, sad ones. Hot, bright and sunny days are delightful. Next, the storm. When the dark side emerges, no voice interaction, quiet, no momentum. No playing time. Warming the bench. Spaced and timed out. Disappearance, no calls, no updates, completely off the radar. You're out of the game, substitute is playing. That close friend, roommate, cousin is the neighbor. When you run, carry your gear with you. Not protected, you may receive the package for life. A gift of mental, physical damage caused by temptation. Run all you want. Your lifeline is ticking. Tick, tick, tick. The sand is failing.

Word of the day:

'Rich'

Reality, Intriguing, Chasing, Harmony

Rich is not just about money. Realizing you have peace within yourself. Success and blessing creates a space where time begins to freeze. New energy to share from love to adventure. Finding chemistry automatically channels back to you. Doors welcome you in. Some handouts can be dangerous. Hallucinations may trap you. Stay true and invest in yourself. Change is not necessary. Informal rejects normal. Smile and be grateful. It keeps you wealthy and ready.

Word of the day:

'Save'

Satisfying, Admiring, Violent, Enemy

Mixing the good with the evil. Character changes are valued indirectly. Picking attributes for your entertainment. No matter how hard you try, something fails. Humans aren't perfectionists, yet materialized. Life shouldn't be taken for granted. It's beautifully crafted in your favor. Challenges and all, there's opportunity for everyone. Be blessed.

Word of the day:

'Fade'

Fading, Absence, Dreadful, Erase

We were close and intimate. You practice, I perfect. Memoires of
laughter, pleasure, and satisfaction. Withdrawal strikes
glancing at the dial-pad wondering if you're holding the phone.
A smile that's reminiscent. 'Been so long. Nothing's the same.
Photos don't apply affection. Choices destroy environments.
Effects are ugly. Time is quiet, chatting is null. Lost while
understanding, the pain is deep. Heart ripping apart.
I'm dying.

Word of the day:

Aids

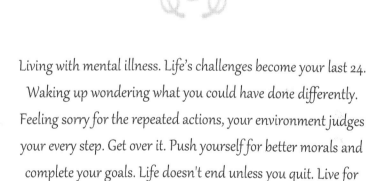

Living with mental illness. Life's challenges become your last 24.
Waking up wondering what you could have done differently.
Feeling sorry for the repeated actions, your environment judges
your every step. Get over it. Push yourself for better morals and
complete your goals. Life doesn't end unless you quit. Live for
the moment. Everyone had this addiction. Love, pray, smile.

Addictions, Insecurities, Delivers, Sacrifice.

Word of the day:

Diamond

Thirty-two years in, and I find a diamond. Thinking that it's nothing until I see the reflection. Beautify crafted rock, as I walk by. Lodged into the pavement attached with a band. The strength of man is not enough to disengage from the ground. I pull physically, mentally, and with great spirits believing anything in life is possible. It will break one day. For now, I'll just breathe and continue the mission in prayer.

Word of the day:

Deaf

Speaking can be judgmental. You can't hear but paying attention to detail is genuine. More focus and alert to body language creates a bond that's unstoppable. Treated fairly, grateful, with no doubts. Seeing the disadvantages you carry, your intelligence is far greater than individuals who are normal.

Giving the opportunity to breathe, live and smile under the same atmosphere, to serve the same purpose. Support, love, and respect. You are human; not a statistic.

Word of the day:

'Crip'

Caring, Really Is Possible

When you hear Crip, normally it's gang ties. They have the same aspects as families. Caring for each other. Always together. Down for whatever. Then colors change the flow. We are one. Same race, same taste, different opinion. We shouldn't kill each other but fight for the king. March like he once did. Educate and share structures for success. Crip all day, one graduation step away.

Word of the day:

'Blood '

Black, Love, Overly, Outdated

Black on black love is mesmerizing. Beautiful shades of colors, tone, and endurance. When well-balanced, we are indestructible. But this generation we tend to have a lack of faith within. Interracial relationships. With respect, it's fine. Yet it breaks up the creation of our image. Procuring money, rather love. Materials, not intelligence. We have them both. We have the anatomy to build a strong foundation together. It takes two. Strong hearts, focus, love, and small amounts of pressure. We shall elevate, brace, gather trust.

Word of the day:

'Side'

Suicide, Is, Dangerous, Energy

Pharmaceuticals, silverware, weapons, choices are endless.
Mental emotion is the deadliest. The act of killing one's self
because depression is constantly first. Self-esteem and sorrow to
follow. Pressure intimates your environment. Cars, bridges,
screaming voices. Just want to end life. Before your calling, cry.
Listen to your soul and ask God to channel in one more time.
His voice, vision, and direction may save you. Spiritually baptize
you as new, pure, fresh son or daughter of man.
Dive into the holy spirit.

Word of the day:

'Full'

Falling, Under, Love, Limit

Time has lapsed. Energy is electrified. High off viability. Smiling is consistent. Never a tedious moment. A wait worth prolonging. Fighting for the impossible. Avoiding all signs without caution. No fear, no remorse. The perfect picture with you in the frame. No flash necessary. Details are exposed. No matter what occurs, reminiscing cannot extract itself. Needs, hunger, craving your addiction. I'm nauseated.

Word of the day:

Guilt

We all make mistakes. No one's perfect. But how we dictate the solution completes the resolution. One day at a time. Guards are high and restrictions maxed. Arguing with silence resolves nothing. Password, emails, technology overwhelming. Basic principals, communication first. Listen with respect and not to respond. Agreeance opens stability. Learn to love, cherish and nurture your significant other. Benefits are welcome after.

Word of the day:

'Drugs'

Drama, Remains, Ugly, Guard, Self

When you repeat your failures, they affect everyone. You may not hear about them but actions will show. Especially if it's outside the circle. Fatal attraction is very real. The eye is in the sky. Thinking you're alone but those satellites are active. Achieving greed, "Winning" but reality shows losing. Slash tires, clothes over the balcony. No reason to continue the doubletake. Find another avenue but fix the door that's left damaged first.

Word of the day:

'Watch'

Watch, Attitude, Tension, Cherish, Her

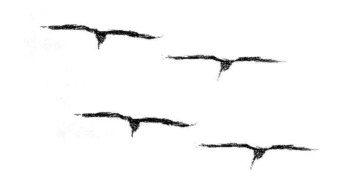

At times we are loud, we shout and don't listen. Disregard your emotions and keep our feet planted. Women have a million traits we cannot understand. We're not meant to. That's woman to man. The other half created to help us. When we fail, they pick us up. Love unconditionally with no limits. Make the impossible practical. Challenges are meaningless. Pressure doesn't exist. Appreciation beyond satisfaction. Love her.

Word of the day:

Money

Green light paper. We never get to see the development process but we put in the hours to make it. Part-time, full-time, overtime. Hard labor, high goals. Great expectations. This material can break everything. Trust, loyalty, relationships and employment. Priorities are demanded with money involved. The love of it is the root of all evil and yet, survival of mankind. Make choices responsibly.

Word of the day:

Users

The nicest people next to you help you when they're available.
They always have handouts. Pretend to support your needs for
their benefits. Asking your schedule before your day starts. But
the moment you fall, they vanish, disappear. No phone calls or
text messages. True colors show. These individuals will corrupt
you. Remove this pessimistic energy away. Cut those snakes'
heads off. They'll respond persistently until acknowledgement
occurs. Let them talk, just don't listen.

Word of the day:

Hammer

When it hits hard, that force is empowered. You have the foreknowledge to understand it's coming. Why do we build unnecessary distractions? Cause and effect. Striking deeper into the wood. Waiting for someone to lift your head. Don't bury yourself. Move out of the way and avoid the metal. Shift your intelligence to stay ahead. Hammer your accomplishments into the wall. Strike and stand tall.

Word of the day:

'Bap'

Business and Personal

That's a hard mix, failures with business can really destroy a
personal relationship. Even though you relate well, it shows
otherwise. It's frustrating at times but what can you do? Push
and improve your work effort and relationships to benefit the
conclusion. The reward will surprise you. Don't take your
attitude indirectly. Same team, same observation. Down to the
last minute. If it's worth it, finish the job.
Work hard, grow together.

Word of the day:

'Meal'

Memories, Evaporate Always, Lonely

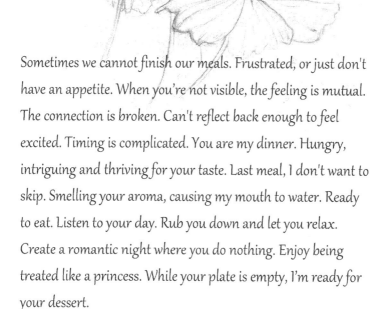

Sometimes we cannot finish our meals. Frustrated, or just don't have an appetite. When you're not visible, the feeling is mutual. The connection is broken. Can't reflect back enough to feel excited. Timing is complicated. You are my dinner. Hungry, intriguing and thriving for your taste. Last meal, I don't want to skip. Smelling your aroma, causing my mouth to water. Ready to eat. Listen to your day. Rub you down and let you relax. Create a romantic night where you do nothing. Enjoy being treated like a princess. While your plate is empty, I'm ready for your dessert.

Word of the day:

'Sleep'

Sex, Lies, Episodes, Envy, Pleasure

Rules. What about them? From the club to the bedroom. That's what counts. Intimate exchanges, one after another. When needs are flamed, times can be arranged. Consequences are fatal. The boomerang effect. How long before your exhibits catch up? Hiding, keeping low. Can't sleep, surroundings are military. Wave the flag and cleanse your soul. Or you will become a part of life's natural habitat. Ground soil.

Word of the day:

'Wet'

Wild, Energy, Tonight

Attack each other. Beauty and the beast. Stimulate the mind, body, and soul. Caress passionately. Everlasting measures. Indoors or exquisite locations. Music in your ears. Seduction at its finest. Lubrication, fruits, and syrups. Start anywhere. Find your direction but don't rush. Longevity is the key. Word play, body language. It's loud and silent. Decipher correctly.

Word of the day:

Words

What we say effect's everything or everyone. Sometimes words are merit by actions and it's hard because situations prevent reality. If only you can hear what I'm feeling. Fighting this intuition eats my heart. Words by tongue or pen. Mentally, just feel me. Listen to how smooth we can be. Words bring bounding respect and closure. Indirectly, they push you away. Close doors and start chaos territory. Your first thought might be wrong but your heart says otherwise. Use your words wisely.

Word of the day:

'Tag'

True, Achievable, Genius

Smarts don't come just from books. Hard work and
determination. Having a plan with goal sets. Staying committed
to yourself. Filtering out distractions while keeping education
balanced. Success structure is 24/7. Lonely but for a purpose.
Financial future with heavy deposit. No paycheck or mail carrier
drop-offs. Living for investments not the moment.

Word of the day:

'Won'

Women, Observe, Necessary

In order to balance a woman, you have to respect them. Love and cater to all her needs. Apply understanding by listening proactively. Affection and effort supports evenly across the relationship. Strengthen her faults and build her confidence. A smart man carries his woman. Wakes her up with greatness. As beautiful as they may seem, women need a male model. Love will complete the package. Make her your best friend. Travel and see beauty together. Bridge the support of happiness and make it everlasting. Persistently, she will make your heart a lifetime.

Word of the day:

'Food'

Fight, Over, Others, Drama

Our ears consume more than our mouths. That's a problem.
We're so busy in everyone's business it becomes a part of our
lives. Spreading rumors, getting physical all over nothing.
Everyone can't be Dr. Phil. Keep your own plate clean.
If your food spills, get your own trash bag.

Word of the day:

Pride

Believe in yourself. Don't let anyone talk down on your life.
Believe in excellences. Smile and do your best at everything.
Pressure should only be formed by you. Jump over the
challenges. Respect and represent yourself positively. There's so
much success around you. Grab enough and feel welcomed.

Push, Relax, Inhale, Determine, Essence

Word of the day:

Life

What do we live for? We stress and take everything for granted.
We are in control of our actions and we hold the weight.
Nothing's promised when we fall asleep. We're very thankful for
the next day. The sun's shining and so should our spirits.
There's no reason to suffer when the answers shouldn't be
questions. The sun should be success, happiness, and blessings.
We hang our heads so low and keep self-discipline. Torturing
the mental illness causing health anxiety. The day is bright but
my vision is dark. I'm not blind, no shades acquired. Sometimes
pain is the outcome for you to gather the forthcoming. Step
outside your body and see everything from all perspectives.
Listen to your heart, follow God and proceed to excellence.

Word of the day:

Homework

Lord knows how much I want to please you and show you the true meaning of desires. Not forcing myself but loving you unconditionally. Breakfast, vacations and everlasting moments. Heaven on earth with you being my angel. Love starts on the left side of my chest and transfers on my right. Right direction, right focus, right woman. What do I need to complete this task? This assignment is confusing but well accepted. Dreams are beautiful but in person, I'm star-struck. Stuttering like I'm having auditions. Glazing from head to toe. I want to start but can't pass go. Grown and aware your standing there. I know I have time, priceless you are. I just care. One day, one second is all I need. Time with you shall set me free. Do you believe me?

Word of the day:

'Spin'

See, Potential, In, Nothing

Sometimes what you find may not be valuable. Could be a collector's item, or just trash. Anything can bring potential to you or someone. A piece of fabric can be dirty but keep the homeless warm. Use your mind to benefit anything. Take time and use your natural talent to magnify an opportunity. Living life, doesn't always end with cost. Priceless is always free. Spread the word and spin today. Don't get nauseous.

Word of the day:

'Death'

Days, Eating, Away, Time, Happening

No one expects to die, especially when you're given a countdown with no control. Randomly you get selected for this job and didn't sign up for. You reflect back on your life wondering what you did wrong. Why me? Fighting this virus. Painfully, mentally unaware of your last moment. Appreciation and faith is all that's left. Love and live happy knowing you got the chance to see light. Your family and friends. Those you've helped alone the path. Cry, but joyfully. Don't let it overwhelm your soul. You were here for a reason and chosen to depart. God loves you. The benefits you brought to Earth was phenomenal. We will always remember who you were and what you stood for. Beautiful human with excellent admiration. While you're still breathing, we love you. Cherish all your memories that hold you forever as one. Never forget you're loved. You're never alone. One love.

Word of the day:

'Gaws'

Grab, A, Woman's, Soul

Women are sensitive. Any second can destroy every emotion.
Fulfill the spirit with love. Show her she's important, beautiful
and valuable. Take her on a date. Buy some roses just because.
Make her priority number 1. She needs a man's energy,
strength, and affection. Surprises are amazing. Stay one step
ahead. Love her from feet to head. Small steps of perfection keep
her heart guessing.

Word of the day:

'Scream'

Soul, Cries, Remembering, Emotional, Addictive, Memory

The maze. We get trapped inside. Finding an exit while rushing is confusing. Conflicts of interest push you in the wrong direction. Frustrated, take a breath. A step back and follow your soul. Negative energy gets you nowhere. You control your destiny. Time is in your favor. God's blessing always available. Don't keep your head down. Get inspired, find inspiration in everything. Cry sometimes. No matter what wall you hit.
An exit is near. Find it.

Word of the day:

Signature

The ink from the pen. Gliding from left to right in a unique pattern. Sketching down your John Doe is famous. But behind that utensil, the most admired individual with positive influences. Your name stands for courage, success, and leadership. A great mentor, scholar and gentleman/woman. A professor of persistence and commitment. The sun that walks the Earth spreading educational morals to the masses. We all need your classes. Just need glasses to stare at the future. Your signature. It's something valuable in every one of us. Life is paper. Sign your formation and cash in responsibly.

Word of the day:

'Dab'

Dreams, And, Blessing

Bright visions every day. We're educators, scholars, and determined individuals. We can see our future. Everything in our hands, our youth, our generation. Dream big. The sky is the limit. Don't get trapped in materialism, money, and negativity. Bless yourself! Set high values for your life. Influence the less fortunate. Spark the brain to change the world. Bless everything in your path. Dab continuously.

Word of the day:

It

Imagine, That

Imagine a world where we have a chance to love one another unconditionally. No hiding, fully open and exposed. Showing your amazing smile to the world and more. Waking up to your adorable view. Kissing and holding you in my arms. It's not fiction anymore. Just passionate commitment. So strong, so healthy. My best friend, lover, and wife. Love you for the rest of my life. Compromise I can now flush away, because I have you every day. Seeing you as I leave, when I return there's more love to achieve.

Word of the day:

Pillow

Soft as hands gliding across the body. When I'm tired, I can depend on you to put me to rest. Hold you in different positions, with comfortable intuition. All day, every night. I never lose sight of you. You never speak disrespectfully. Cause any concern. Just pleasure to urn. A sensation with smiles of graduation.

Word of the day:

'Can't'

Creative, Ambitions, Naturally, Timed

Never really paid attention to this word until I met you. I can't hold you, can't love you, can't lay with you. Can't make you smile with passion attached. There's so many limitations like I'm on probation. Just an amazing sensation for one occupation. To make you achieve the energy you never received. Absolute happiness. Waking up to a laughter only I can see. A glance in your beautiful eyes, creates a smile and a surprise. I can only be wise. For now, I just mark the calendar days and stay prayed. Maybe one day. **Creative, Ambitions, Naturally, Timed.**

Word of the day:

Athlete

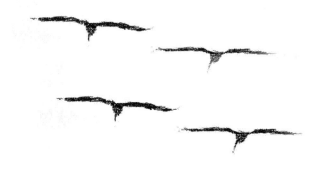

You sleeping again without me. Wrapped around in a blanket that captures all your energy. Surrounding you with warmth and compassion. Touching your silky soft, gentle skin. Back in this state of mind. Left on the side, not drafted. Practice daily, work hard to enter the game. I take my first step forward and get red-shirted. Hate practice. Pain and agony. Just a tragedy. Can't continue to play number two. Unwillingly, I quit striving to start living. My court, new rules. My building.

Time to change. Gear up.

Word of the day:

Wishbone

Beauty and pain on each side. The closer you move one way, the pressure break occurs. Different grasps effect flexibility, opportunity, actuality. Presentations generate anxious tendencies. Seduction barriers raise the arc, creating a sound of destruction. Decisions fight as questions. Do I persuade with confidence? Bite the bullet and lean back. Tick for tack. That's the crack. Which side is light? Either left or right.

A squeeze too tight.

Word of day:

'Rag'

Real, Attention, Genuine

Trust is where it starts. Build a wall of importance. Stay true
with everything. Facts are always valid. Actions speak louder
than words, the fabrication of void. Understand the meaning of
loyalty. The drive pushes you to discover your opportunities of
happiness. Gratitude expands you to want more. Interest in the
mind, body, and soul. Grow old as one. A destiny, beautiful
foundation in all situations. Life is a priceless vacation. Take a
flight with love every night. Love is your sight. It may be bright,
push you left. but your heart is right.

Word of the day:

Kid

Regardless how much a gentleman you can be; it's never enough. The damage from a fractured past carries toward any man's future potential. Introduction is a compromise checklist rather than interest and respect. The elephant in the room. Chasing away grateful opportunities. Honest men can never understand a woman's emotion but the pain is viable. Some of us care, love, and respect women. Just don't treat us like kids.

Keeping It Distant.

Word of the day:

Black

Couldn't say that word any better. The meaning is so deep.
Everything we stand, march, and stood for. Strength of a lion,
heart of a warrior. Success is a breath of fresh air we embellish.
Fight through the rainy days, but shine brighter every day.
Rights to education, sports with astonishing presentations.
Valued brilliance at its peak. Endurance too strong to act weak.
We'll never be in defeat. Changed focus in 2009, has over 1
million on Obama's front line. MLK journey one last time.
All as one, we are one of a kind.
Beautiful, Loving, Amazing, Charming, Kings.

Word of the day:

'Give'

Gather, Information, Value, Exit

Time to stop giving. Nothing wrong with saying no. Gather
yourself and realize, if you're not receiving the same in return,
that's the end game! Regardless how nice or grateful the
moment is. A trained eye knows. Feeding off your energy. One
sided exchanges. You're just the client, last option for
emergency. Draw the line and notice the change in behavior.
If the outcome's recognized, then the reflection is neutral.
Justify the truth. Time is on your side. Stop wasting it.

Word of the day:

Kite

Relationships can dwell. Spice up the situation. Take some risk and gamble anonymously. Surprises are creative. Switch up the routine. Pay attention to the signs and emotional language. Gifts at work, tighter communication. Mind stimulation. Try not to support only yourself. Shine as one, have some fun. Picture perfect moments are great. Even if you don't like an event, enjoy the company. **Keep, Interest, Timing, Everything**.

Word of the day:

'Fish'

First, Intuition, Surprises, Him

Snap your fingers and here we are. A new testament of happiness, I'm willing to try. We know the faults, we have experience. Our direction is positive. No value of money or event is determined. Just a pretty smile and time caters everything. Small steps will last a long way. Laughing and bounding I'm here to stay. Treat you with honesty, open your door and appreciate listening to you. Two hearts, one mine, fresh start about time. Dinner with no roof, stars bright above. Body so warm, a hug tighter than a glove. Spoiled to have you alone. I'm chosen, blessed to be in your zone. Cold air and sand, walking while holding your hand. A beautiful plan with little demand. Unbelievable view, clear water and just us two. You inhale a deep breath and I exhale for you. A kiss is just the beginning, sinning, not worried about winning. Just so real to play the cards you deal. My heart is a steal. I'm dying for this day, so here's my will. A silent kill.

Word of the day:

Left

The heart is a dangerous place. Wants and desires, around you, it's on fire. Beginning to departed myself. Painful but a substantial direction. Your strides don't accelerate your reflection. I'm a human being with character, not a tool. Our lives are real and so are the rules. Valuable memories wasted. Time ago, reality came and faced it. Alive and alert, ready to bury the dirt. Life hurts, but I'm not dead. More cautions with the heart instead of guessing with the head.

Leaving, Everything, Fictitious, Toxic.

Word of the day:

'Stress'

Serious, Tension, Release, Energy, Somehow, Safely

A balloon filled builds up with air, wishing we can pop. Rather from work or life's experience. Take a sec' and breathe. Mental challenges which you can bare. Adding fuel to the fire can cause anxiety attacks. Reroute the aggression for positive selection. It's just a testament. Your time here on Earth is short. Smile and enjoy the journey. Don't dig a hole to bury yourself. Walk around the obstacles proudly. Your potential never makes you a failure. It shows who you really are. Strong, past the scars. You're a star.

Word of the day:

'Post'

Pray, Overwhelming, Suffering, Testimony

Lord I'm ready to jump. I don't have enough fight in me to push forward. I see your swimming pool of faith and even though I can't swim, I know you're not going to let me drown. I need to follow your light so I can understand your connection, your vision, your direction. Stress, pulling me apart. I don't want anyone's energy if it's evil. Makes me dark with hatred. I want the pure life with persistent goals of pressure. Nothing given but striving for blessings taken. No more waiting, no more trying. My back is on the edge. Last inhale, hopefully my wings depart while I'm falling through the sky. My first and last cry. I tried. I just died. Forgive me, father. Lack of thinking, I didn't bother.

Word of the day:

Music

You're like a vinyl record. I love listening to you but everyone wants to play your track. They like your instrumental. The way you shake your beats. Watching your drums vibrate, communicates feedback. I glance at the record but it's that special edition. Platinum untouched and protected for your eyes only. I want to grab it. Hold it so right, till I brake it. Listen to the melody, caress the track. Become breathless by the second verse. Head attached to the hook, makes me wanna' dip the needle for a mix. Change the mood to maximize the groove. Drop this new record for a rewarding attitude. Bodies in twist, repeat is the kiss. Vibe is up, can't silence you down. Want this music on forever, if silence were finished with a new sound. Would be nice to make a record together. But after you keep releasing platinum singles, your wait time seems never. I may change from Rap to RnB. Real admirable person waiting for refreshing, nice, beautiful woman. Guarantee.

Word of the day:

Map

We were born into life; no guidelines, directions, or instructions. Challenges with race, religion and life-changing decisions. When in doubt, quitting is the easy way out. Fading away from everything. Conflicts make you progress. providing a better future than your predecessor. Stamping your name in vain. Branding for your culture. Such a beautiful sculpture. Be thankful for each breath, each day. Tomorrow if you wake up lost, always remember to pull out your map.

Make, Anything, Possible

Word of the day:

Space

A Special person who resembles a diamond. Precious, unique and incredible. Regardless of the distance, it's exciting. Itching to see you again. An addition that keeps me relapsing. Passionate spirit that bounds so evenly. Pushes inspiration for tomorrow. Picture perfect processing. Waiting for you to develop opportunities. Amazingly, your charm never turns off. Solar powered by God's strength from the sun. Glowing even where stars are glistening. Soft library voice, I'm listening. Challenges worth the fight. Even if it takes our whole lives. Your vision is my sight. A man, with a friend, maybe a wife. A deep swallow puts us at thrust. Love is strong, sometimes a curse.

Exotic taste from the face. Fashion so bold, a model is resembled. Luck can't define your definition. Time will put me within your intuition. You're the meal, my nutrition. Ready for submission. This menu has various offers. Gladly, I have reservations. Sitting at this glorious location. You remain my vacation. I'm waiting...

Word of the day:

Tea

Made of precious leaves from an incredible harvest. Smell and
taste that's unbearable. The aroma quenches your thirst.
Vibrations of sweat running down your face. Flexing for your
glass. An acrobatic beverage with desires to swallow. My body
temperature rises above caution. An elegant shaped atmosphere
waiting to be filled. Ready to release my juice inside the pitcher.
The taste is passionate; fresh, sour lemons. Add honey and ice.
Bring on the spice. Sipping slowly while enjoying your
everlasting. Started at the top, heading toward the bottom. All
out of energy till the last drop. Falling out the glass, landing on
a hotspot. Touching, Everything, Available. What tea are you
having tonight? Dark.

Word of the day:

'Foil'

Feeling, Oblivious, Irritated, Lust

The gray area. Wrapped up inside emotions. Confined by the heart, connections are rejections. Constantly, I see something within your spirit, but frustrated because I'm still holding you. Not knowing what direction to start. Failing to understand why it hurts so much. Believing, showing you the truth. Blinded by my love, I'm ready to leave this Earth. Opportunity wasn't granted from the start. Time to wake up and depart. New attire, fresh boots. I must March. It's better that I don't see you. Favorite time of day is dark. Need to find myself, grab a paddle, journey and sail. Noah's Arc. Cold and alone, but my heart rushes with blood. While the planet get flushed by the ocean, I float across the flood. One love.

Word of the day:

Coin

Collectors' items come in different shapes and sizes. Various choices. Accent, young, beautiful and historic. Remastered models have superior appeal but the value isn't efficient. Gold, copper and silver, all designed by hand. Everyone's held this impeccable metal. Changes the way we live life. Just as important as love. By reference, love is intangible occasionally. Estimating coins toward love has no revenue. But the heart generates faith, trust, and eternity. Can't be placed in a purse nor wallet. Walking up next to your beautiful spouse, children or family. Amazing smiles, laughter, first word. Love is so unheard. Until you experience this excellence, keep searching. It's out there. Just don't use all your coins to buy love. Never for sale. Just an exchange with another investor.

Word of the day:

'Bills'

Bothered, Irritated, Lonely, Lost, Soul

Everything is falling apart. Losing family and friends over priorities. Health creates separations, missed events and sadness. Nothing is intentional. But missing your moment is a dramatic failure. Realizing you're inspired by my steps, a role model who continues to break emotion. I can see darkness forming in your eyes. Not the enemy, but I feel like a terrorist. Honest person with actions destroying important elements with destruction. Wanted only in California. A state we shared journeys together. Apologies, excuses cannot be fixed with words. Time, love and affection is your reflection. Standing in the mirror, only seeing myself. No one's alone. Missed the stage, lights and your outcomes. Forgiveness so hard to understand when given the last opportunity. Where does that leave me? Striving for another chance? You've been reading this book forever. May you still include me in your chapters. Through thick and thin, I'm trying to win. Please don't end when ... we can still begin.

Word of the day:

'God'

Gifted, Opportunity, Daily

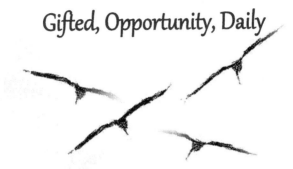

Sometimes you may not feel like you're special. Starting your day to repeat over, tomorrow. Frustrated about your life's goals and always trying, without progress. Quitting is envy. Your talent is buried within your soul. Following your heart and exposing that gift will grant you success. Pray to find understanding. Believe that anything is possible. Don't ignore the signs. The positive strives of information you share can become beneficial for your future. If you don't accomplish developments today, God will create opportunities daily, and bless you to see tomorrow. There's success in pain. You have to let go of what you like and follow what you love. Even if you're alone. You have God.

Word of the day:

Solo

Alone with time to wake up. A drastic change for the best.
Smart, independent star waiting to shine across the sky.
Nothing wrong with spreading your wings and soaring through
the universe. Beautiful horizon every morning. Room to
accomplish remarkable standards. Painful past leads to joyful
adventures tomorrow. The creature will guide you. Listen
closely, and bring obstacles with less tension. Follow the voice,
senses and heart. The brain will spark. Just a matter of time.
Single, Only, Life, Option.

Word of the day:

'Glue'

Glamorous, Love, Unbelievable, Experience

Never thought a man would be linked to one individual. Different and unique. Your spirit gravitates my uprising. Challenging myself, displaying educated matters and non-indulgent sequences. Patiently waiting for your arrival. Vibes that honor internal fire. Fascinating, blessed to have such a strong back-bone. I value my heart to you. Eat, pray, love and stay. With you it's every day. No matter how many stones hit me, your aide completes my healing. God's will shows me the sky is blue. The hearts are red and love is true. I thank you for all the years, tears and becoming my glue. What a clue. Only from you.

Word of the day:

Scope

Your vision is the point of sight. Everything doesn't start clear.
You may have to move objects from a path to gain focus. Close
some doors, breathe slowly and achieve determination.
Distractions are an addiction. Giving your input on useless
incentives draws road blocks. Intelligence comes from the mind
but your handouts cannot benefit everyone's request. There's
pain from rejection, yet prosperity within self. Intelligent people
navigate in silence. Yet the outcome from progress is
aggressively loud. Start with yourself, finish with confidence.
When life graduates, tears of passion may run freely.

Stop, Crying, Over, People, Everyday.

Word of the day:

'Bust'

Better, Understand, Serious, Tension

Sometimes, we give off bad energy or expressions that cause a conflict of interest. Doesn't happen intentionally, yet response is high. Arguing and fighting doesn't resolve anything. Find a positive solution and place all factors on the table. Process of elimination. Listen to both sides. Mixing the good and the bad. React with kindness. If you over judge your boundaries. It's OK to apologize. Better to remain the bigger individual and stand tall. Never belittle yourself. Healthy perception keeps you in good favor with your peers. Saves all the stress and tears. Annihilate the fear. Learn from the mistakes and ... awake a better person.

Word of the day:

Sex

Tension and suspension. Physicality is the last place it begins.
Unwinding your visionary. Absorbing your fragrance, fantastic
physique and intelligence. Nothing sexier than an individual
with enlightenment. Beliefs don't follow materialistic vision. The
will to hold your own. Accomplishments are your sin. Elevation
to the highest level. Landing business deals to completing that
doctorates degree. That's a true calling. Those are the desires a
real man supports. A woman with determination, not a
nomination. Glamorous model who thinks outside the bottle.
Believes in natural health while others squeeze, vomit to remain
hollow. I applaud your cloud. Stay successful and keep
screaming loud. Your results are 'Wow'!

Word of the day:

Fag

Nerds say silent and alone. The strongest focus on absorbing intellectual instruction. Very crafty, articulate. Judgement of character doesn't deprive their beliefs. Drawing abuse from jealous, envious types. Communication was never expressed verbally. But the amazing results are alarming. The most quiet person invented the next-wave revolution of technology. Everyone becomes your spectator. Sparking life, changing perspective on goals. Follow your heart regardless of how or what barrier transpired. Inspiration is just time. A figment of your dream. Creativity begins with yourself. Better to be different. Craftsmanship will **Finally, Achieve, Greatness.**

Word of the day:

'Goat'

Greatness, Offers, Amazing, Talent

Push everything to your max. Some days there's no time for sleep. Yet seeing progress complete is blissful. Establishing a foundation for the youth. A tall wall to climb over. Expressing anything possible. Judgement will come. Distractions play no part but emotion. Painful filter being alone. Success starts with heart. No entourage or walk in the park. Stand out and provide excellence in your profession. God shall have your blessing. Expand your knowledge using planners, charts, organizers. Kills for second guessing. Deliver the message. To be smart, is to be different. To see the finished line, continue to race against yourself. Practice makes perfection.

Word of the day:

Dinner

The food looks amazing. The aroma is memorizing, but I'm locked into you. Beautiful and exciting to be with me. Watching you glow from head to toe. Endless conversations. Happiness without forcing impressions. Being natural. As the food remains untouched. My voice continues to build your smile. Goosebumps start to arrive and I'm not surprised. Cold and not shy. Hypothesis by your sparkling eyes. Sharing a toast because we're so close. Such pride from two individual people. Your heart is always welcome to this type of sequel.

Word of the day:

Bookmark

In life, we tend to have a place marker. A reflection that reminds us to return back. Read through the acceptance of sacrifices. Chapters that are challenging but divided into small journeys. We conquer one and turn the pages that follow. The longer you're breathing, the prolonging of this exhibit persists. You will never comprehend the language given. Just continue turning till you finish. Place your book of knowledge on the shelf and find another adventure to endeavor. If you pause, just remember, "It's ok. I have enough today." Mark this chapter and continue with honor, wisdom and integrity.

Word of the day:

Pain

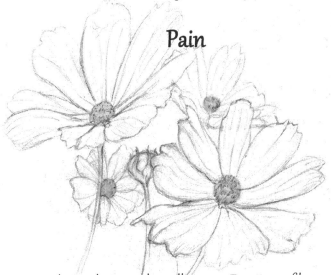

Pain doesn't hurt until we allow it to. Emotions of love and trust. Knowing ahead the guilt of fault. Why are the wants so important? They bring stress, anxiety, and a variety of diseases. Just for one word, "please." Asking yourself: what more can I do? The only problem you have is acknowledgement. Space away and listen to your soul. If you can sum your inquiries independently, why involve the next attribute? Control your own character. You're the leader. Follow only the heart. If you see the light, that's a good spark. Even when times are dark.

Fulfill your chart. **Pass, Annoying, Ignorance, Nonsense**

Word of the day:

'Rules'

Relapsing, Under, Love, Endless, Sex

We love to break them. Sampling that irresistible platter. Rules don't matter. Kissing, touching, lusting every ounce of your body. Vibrations and penetration. Ignored calls till the night falls. Watching you crawl, while my jaw's on pause. Discovering all your channels. Pressing the guild button. Switching categories while enjoying this glory. Fantasy and reality in the same story, with minutes left in this show. You have to depart to a home you must go to. I'll continue to adjust this antenna to find your episode. Holding the control, waiting for updates to unfold. Till next season...

Word of the day:

'Rope'

Reality, Observation, Pass, Experience

As the world turns, the past still remains the new reflection.
Segregation of race, religion, and sex. Equality seem shattered.
Broken beliefs of glass cutting into the souls of millions. When
standing your ground gets you red-shirted. Slammed on
classrooms floors. Or surrendering to a fatal, heartless
execution. The pain starts a resolution. Voices are ignored only
by the privileged. The educated scholar with inspirational,
structural, powerful vocabulary, still can't overturn the eyes and
acknowledgement of the system. Our ancestors gave us the will
power to survive. We shall continue to fight, achieve and die for
our next generational youth. For one day, thou shalt know ...
the truth.

Word of the day:

Says

Smoke, Away, Your, Stress

Watching your actions in the clouds. Deep breaths and exhales. Feel better when released. Rather continuing to be angry. Take a puff. Spark a flame and enjoy your lane. Weed or nicotine goes straight to the brain. Internal pain will drive you insane. Don't hurt yourself. Get spaced out someplace else. Visualize a vacation of a beautiful location. Let your smoke become the camera and the lighter insert the film. Snap those memories of pleasure. Life and love, the only solution you have to measure. Finish till you peek. Close your eyes and enjoy a harmonizing sleep.

Word of the day:

Jump Rope

It takes a pair of hands to contribute to the game. Without progression, a stand still will have you abandoned. As the ropes turn, an interest of relations grow. Opportunities are welcomed. Equality in togetherness, happiness, and success will maintain your partner. Turning your new hands of time while the opposite direction unwinds. Seeing no one jumping in the middle. The end of the rope is a segment of beauty. Pulling you closer as I tug for your love. Realizing we can still hop as one. Let's live life, jump soon. Remove the rope and replace a broom. Beautiful place, more room. See you there, one afternoon

Word of the day:

Bartender

Everyone wants something from you but I just need a moment of your time. Coming to visit because I see something inspiring in your eyes. Several voices ask for your attention. I wish they all were on suspension. We connect like a parallel line. Beautiful smile as I wait patiently for my wine. Trying not to be a follower so I wait for your lead. Too bad you're not clocked out, so you can sit next to me. Introduction including exchanges of names and pleasant vocabulary. Channels of love flowing through the air outside of February. Limitations and boundaries occur at this location. Maybe one day, a new start. A more phenomenal situation. For now, I will accept this probation unit we change stations. I'm patience.

Word of the day:

Stripper

Judging a book by its cover. Strong words to condone an intelligent mother. Naturally talented, single supported system. Born into this world with no help. A mouth to feed. Crying within while mentally angered, steamed. Don't look down on yourself. This is just an occupation to help with college tuition. When the leverage is balanced, your education will bless your success. Your story will change lives for women to understand anything's possible! Nothing's an obstacle! Stand tall with your master's in your left, daughter on your right. Tears of joy with smile so bright. Preaching God's might. Devastation surrounds your gift. As long as you're willing to break free, progress is the light you shall see. Time is key. Heart equals free.

Word of the day:

Talk

Second time around but everything feels so brand new. From being in your presence to bringing you presents. Exciting when you see belief within me. Learning how to be simple, soft and gentle. Expanding my mental and absorbing your temple. A beautiful palace I get to establish. Your smile's extraordinary and matches your piano-symphony voice. With you I have a choice. Try Another Love and pray with bended knee. Because you would kill to miss what the heart can't see.

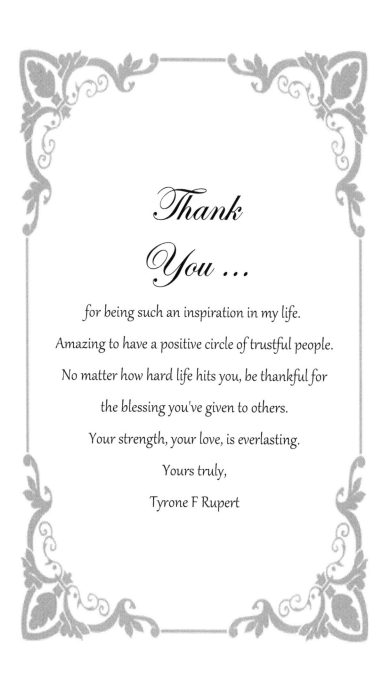

Thank You ...

for being such an inspiration in my life.

Amazing to have a positive circle of trustful people.

No matter how hard life hits you, be thankful for

the blessing you've given to others.

Your strength, your love, is everlasting.

Yours truly,

Tyrone F Rupert

Miesha

A Memorizing, Irresistible, Entertaining, Satisfying, Happy,
Adorable woman. You, my friend, have accomplished so much
in life. From traveling the world, to blessing the world, a
handsome young man; the split image of perfection that pushes
you to greater heights. A smile that makes you speechless
because happiness had no sound. A character which cannot be
duplicated. Charismatic at all times. Personality is zero to none.
A very well crafted gem made of potential.
Special, special, special.

J.J.

A different twist in direction but so inspiring to be around.
Creativity is second nature to your habitat. From fashion to
laughing, your company never grows old. So young at heart,
your mother's smiling at the perfect example of how you
continue to spread love to the world. Channeling out all
negative energy into the J.J. spirit. We all know when you speak.
We will hear it. Thankful for your friendship.
Truly and sincerely, Ty.

Minerva Smith

From funny to inspirational. Your strength goes on for miles. A woman that display no signs of quitting, guilt, fault, and remains uplifting. Your company is spiritual. A poised individual with gratitude. You can never have a carbon copy. The finest at bringing peace from within everybody. Regardless of the updated timestamp given, your family and friends will always love you, respect you, represent you forever.

Much love, Ty.

Vinnie

You're taking away all the muscles from the young men. Year by year, you shed a tear in the mirror. Looking at yourself, blessed how your life has developed with God, giving you the tools to provide for your entire family, and even save your own blood. You fight like no other man on this planet. You are the strongest black man in every factor. Faith, love, and family. All the teachings you've blessed me were outstanding. You offer so much security. Stay guarded, humble and remain ...

the man of God.

Tatiana

Africa inside the United States. Beautiful, star-stuck, and jaw-
dropping. Trapped inside your glow. Understanding how
flawless you are. Educated, respectful, talented and true.
Incredible energy releases when surrounded by you. The perfect
smile. A diamond, memorized by all angles. Such a selection of
perfection that keep the mind guessing. A thankful blessing to
have your presence.

Mothers

The most influential woman on the planet! Objectively, work
has no limits. From giving birth to raising a garden, cooking,
working two or more jobs. Her labor ethic is unimaginable.
Tasking is effortless. Strong-willed and precious. Making the
impossible---feasible. Constructed at heart, a war-zone mind
and a soul silent to the wind. Glamorous and bright, as if the
sun has no light. Without you in our lives, we have no sight.

Dorothy Alls

The most amazing woman on this planet. Taught me everything about the game and to remain strong. Raised her three children alone. Brilliant mentor and enjoyable friend. I'll never look past you. I thank you for bringing me onto this Earth, to find my path. Your intelligence and respect shifted beautifully in my direction. From knee-high to grown man, you were definitely in God's plan. I love you and appreciate your loyalty as a woman, and mother. Thank you for leading the way for me.

The Ruperts

No matter the conditions we sacrificed, we always find a way to stay together. I love all of you guys! Taught me how to be strong, laugh and love. Home after home, I was never alone. Learning to fight, expand the mind, it took one family member at a time.

Clayton, your drive showed me ways to never stop moving. An educated mind is powerful.

CJ, no matter how many times the doors close, your pride is so high and faith so strong!

Cemar, injuries stopped you from joining to the Dallas Cowboys but you are the number one quarterback a brother can have, tossing me knowledge only blood can understand. No longer am I playing running back, I'm coaching thanks to you!

Deidra, a mother of war. The tank guarding her soldiers against the nation. They love you so much. Providing a home, rooms and growth for their generation. You're a sensation!

DeMesha, your mind is free. Keep everything true.
Rather it being loud or silent you give me advice to try it.
My family tree ....
The youngest root expressing his love for us.
Thank you again. Amen.

Anthony Bowens

A true blessing of a best friend. Connected from a word search
through Craigslist. How amazing technology brings people
together. I appreciate you as a person and thankful for helping
me manage, at the lowest times of my life. You never neglected
or disrespected. Positive father-figure and hard-working
husband to your wife. Your guideline of persistence is excellent.
May God continue to shine his light above your halo. Pray
before we sleep, waking up with his shield surrounding the
family.

Sincerely, Ty

Janice Freeman

Without you, this book would never have seen the day off light. I'm so thankful that you've entered my life. Your perspective on women has changed so much of my vision, through the spirit.

You showed me the true meaning of strength, passion and determination. Your sensation to strive seems effortless, but the progress of work empowers what a woman can be. Continue to be the gateway, the light. And smile as bright as heaven. Angels exist but you have to believe in order to see. I see you. Fly away.

Made in the USA
San Bernardino, CA
11 February 2018